GET THE TAXMAN OFF YOUR BACK

DIRK B. DANOS CPA, CTRS

Copyright © 2018 Dirk B Danos CPA, CTRS

No part of this book may be reproduced or transmitted in any form or by any means without prior written permission of the author and publisher. All rights reserved.

All rights reserved.
ISBN: 9781726883412
ISBN-13:

Formatting by Kristen Forbes, deviancepress.com

Dirk B Danos Contact Information

www.irscrisishelp.com

1-800-433-0986 (24 Hours)

PO Box 7052

Belle Chasse LA 70037

LIABILITY DISCLAIMER

The material in this manual is general in nature and is not intended as specific advice on any particular matter. The author and publisher expressly disclaim any and all liability to any persons whatsoever in respect of anything done by any such person in reliance, whether in whole or part, on the book. While the author and publisher are engaged in rendering tax advice and representation, the author and publisher are not engaged in rendering career advice, legal advice or financial services. Any services, references, and/or websites that may be mentioned are provided for informational purposes only. Please take appropriate legal and/or professional advice before acting on any information in this manual. Tax law changes frequently, do not rely on the material herein as current law.

To my beautiful daughters Emily and Ava. I love you more than my capacity for expression. I am so proud of you!

The author takes limited new clients per month.
Call 800-433-0986 (24 Hours) or visit www.irscrisishelp.com
to schedule an appointment.

CONTENTS

Introduction	xi
1. How Did I Get into This Mess?	1
2. There Is Definitely a Problem	7
3. The Taxpayer Bill of Rights	13
4. Do It Yourself or Hire a Professional	39
5. Resolution Starts with Compliance	45
6. Statute of Limitations	49
7. Currently Non-Collectable	53
8. Penalty and Interest Abatement	55
9. Bankruptcy	63
10. Offer in Compromise	67
11. Installment Agreements	75
12. What You Need to Know About Audits	83
Afterword	91
Acknowledgments	93

INTRODUCTION

Initially, I took tax resolution clients into my practice to level off the seasonality of tax return work. But the more cases I worked, the more I realized I'd found my calling. I found it gratifying to help decent, hard-working people solve their tax problems. I was able to remove a burden that had kept them up at night, had forced them to work extra hard to catch up, and had stolen time away from the activities and people they loved.

If you are struggling in silence with an IRS tax problem, then I wrote this book for you! I want to offer you hope that your problems *can* be resolved once and for all. You can be freed from the bondage of IRS forced collection. There is a better way!

I encourage you to get the help you need. The information in this book will give you an awareness of the programs available for resolving any IRS non-compliance issue. You will also discover what rights you are afforded by the Internal Revenue Code. But I don't want to give you the idea that you won't be able to handle your own case—that's not the point here. I'm simply offering a message of hope and a basic understanding of the process. This will enable you to find the right person to solve your problem.

If you finish this book and are still at a loss for direction, contact my office for more help. Although I take a limited number of cases per month, I would be glad to hear from you and offer you some excellent referrals. Imagine how you would feel if you were placed in the hands of a competent expert who deals with the IRS on a regular basis and who REALLY CARES about helping YOU!

1

HOW DID I GET INTO THIS MESS?

It probably isn't your fault that you're in this situation. And as you read this book, remember that there *is* a solution for you. Sometimes, bad things just happen to good people. After all, you didn't plan to run short of cash just when the tax payment was due. When life-changing events occur, your focus shifts and tax compliance is the last thing on your mind. It is an all too common occurrence which results from irregular income, an interruption in income, divorce, forgiveness of debt, or even poor financial advice.

While there are hundreds of factors that can contribute to your tax problem, let's discuss those which are the most common. You'll quickly see that this widespread issue is not unique to you. In fact, according to the most recent IRS Data Book, there are over 19 million taxpayers who owe money to the IRS. That equates to about one in every fifteen people.

IRREGULAR CASH FLOW

Self-employed business owners often experience cash flow problems, which pressure the owner to decide which obligations are the most urgent. If the owner doesn't pay the employees, they'll stop coming to work, thereby shutting down business operation. The same is true for vendors that the business depends on for critical resources. Therefore, a common solution to cash flow deficiency is to pay the employees and vendors while postponing tax payment. This is a very slippery slope that gets out of control quickly. To make matters worse, the IRS doesn't detect the situation until much later, allowing the problem to grow. Often the problem goes undetected for 3 years or more. By the time the IRS commences enforced collection, the problem has gotten massive.

UNEMPLOYMENT

Interruption in income can originate for many reasons: disability, layoffs, family illness, and many others. No matter the cause, this interruption creates a difficult situation for the taxpayer, who is trying desperately to maintain their family's welfare. As a result, tax payments can be forgotten or ignored.

The taxpayer may also be forced to draw money out of a 401k or IRA account to make ends meet. But this becomes problematic when the next tax return is filed, and the tax amount due is too much to afford. A vicious cycle of non-compliance due to unpaid tax or unfiled returns begins.

DIVORCE

Filing Status

A divorce can result in many unexpected tax liabilities. For instance, an employee has tax withheld from their paychecks based upon the married filing status for the entirety of 2018. But then their divorce is finalized in late December 2018, requiring a filing status of single for their 2018 tax return. All year, the taxes were under-withheld at the lower married status rate, creating a significant balance due.

Alimony

When a spouse begins receiving alimony and is unaware that this new form of income is taxable, there is an unexpected, large tax payment due with the return filing.

Settlements

Divorce settlements often require property to be converted to cash, which triggers a taxable event and a large tax balance due.

Sometimes, a combination of these events occur, and they're happening at a time when the taxpayer is incurring significant expenses to re-establish a new life. This happens even with cordial divorces, but if there is animosity from one or both spouses, it gets even worse.

DEBT FORGIVENESS

Many people are unaware of the following rules and get caught with a surprise tax bill. A cancellation of debt due to property being abandoned, foreclosed, or repossessed is treated by the IRS as taxable income. So, after you have your house foreclosed or vehicle repossessed, the IRS increases the pain by asking you to pay a tax for losing it. WOW! If this seems unfair to you, I feel the same. Nonetheless, this is yet another way an unsuspecting taxpayer can fall behind.

As you can see, most tax trouble starts when the taxpayer is unable to pay the tax due. Maybe you planned to catch up after some anticipated or unanticipated event occurred, changed your cash position, and forced you to skip one tax payment. But then the next tax payment is due and cash is still tight, so you skip yet another tax payment, again planning to catch up later. Or maybe you are completely surprised by an unexpected tax bill you can't afford to pay. Whatever the reason, and there are hundreds more, you did not intend to get into this trap.

As time goes on, the tax return filing deadline approaches and you still can't catch up. It becomes more difficult, since now there are multiple payments required to get current. You decide to avoid filing (which is the worst thing to do), since you are unable to pay the taxes. You think that if you file the return, the IRS will "find you out," and you're not ready to pay the tax or answer all their questions right now. This cycle quickly compounds into an insurmountable problem which results in multiple years of unfiled returns and a mountain of unpaid tax.

Here is the reality of the situation. There are many programs available to you for regaining your compliance with the IRS. Most don't even require you to pay all the tax due. You just need to arrange to pay it systematically or come to some form of settlement agreement. All of the programs require you to file the unfiled returns though. Failing to file a tax return when it's due is a misdemeanor. Owing the IRS money is not. Even if you do not have the records required to file the return, don't fret because there are many solutions to this problem as well.

It doesn't matter how you went off the rails with IRS compliance, there is a resolution option for your situation. Again, it's not your fault, but you do have to fix it and time is not on your side here. Every day that you do nothing, the problem gets exponentially worse with the daily compounding of interest and assessment of harsh penalties.

ALWAYS FILE THE RETURN!

There are two types of IRS penalties of concern to individual taxpayers: failure to pay, and failure to file. The failure to pay penalty is calculated by adding 0.5% of the tax due amount per month to your account. The failure to file penalty is calculated by adding 5% of the tax due amount per month. So the failure to file penalty is **10 times more** than the failure to pay penalty. The bottom line? Always FILE THE RETURN!

What if you have no records to file the return with? You may be under the untrue assumption that you cannot file a return. I am happy to inform you that these records are available even if they aren't in your possession. The IRS can produce a document called a wage and income transcript for every taxpayer. It shows nearly everything you will need in order to file the return. The rest of the information can be collected elsewhere, like from your bank and credit card statements. You're even allowed to make reasonable estimates of amounts. Again, I remind you to FILE THE RETURN!

Remember that there IS a solution for your tax problem!

2

THERE IS DEFINITELY A PROBLEM

What's the big deal if I don't file a tax return?

Not filing a legally required tax return is a crime punishable by one year of jail time and a $10,000 fine per unfiled return. That's right—it's a crime to not file your tax return if you're required to file one. If this doesn't motivate you to file the return, you may be incentivized by the reduction in penalties. Remember, the failure to file penalty is 5% of the tax due per month, whereas the failure to pay penalty is 0.5% of the tax due per month. This means that the IRS will penalize you tenfold more severely for not filing versus not paying. YOU SHOULD ALWAYS FILE YOUR TAX RETURNS.

STATUTE OF LIMITATIONS

The filing of a tax return begins the statute of limitations process. The statute for assessment is the amount of time the IRS is allowed by law to assess a tax, which is three years from the date that the return is filed, or the due date of the return. Once assessed, the IRS then has a 10-year statute of limitations to collect the tax. If they fail to collect within the 10-year statute, collection is barred by law. The statute of limitations calculation has many caveats that make it difficult to accurately determine. As a result, the IRS is often incorrect about a taxpayer's statute of limitations date, making the IRS think there is still time to collect the tax when legally they cannot. Although no one knows for sure, the estimate is that 40% of the statute dates calculated by the IRS are wrong. This quagmire within the system has saved many taxpayers. YOU SHOULD ALWAYS FILE YOUR TAX RETURNS.

What if you were due a refund but did not file? Obviously you will not get the refund, and you are also subject to a statute of limitations. The refund statute of limitations is the later of three years from the date the return was filed, or two years from the date the tax was paid. If you failed to file a return, then the statute of limitations is two years from the date the tax was paid. If you fail to file a return within this timeframe and are due a refund, you are barred from receiving it. In this instance you have just made a generous donation to your federal government. YOU SHOULD ALWAYS FILE YOUR TAX RETURNS.

One of the resolution options for taxpayers at odds with the IRS is to have tax debt discharged through a bankruptcy case. As I will explain later, if you do not file the tax return, then the tax due on that return, along with any penalties and interest, are not eligible for discharge with your other debts. So, by failing to file the tax return, you eliminate one of your options for resolution. This can be the quickest and least expensive option. By the way did I mention that YOU SHOULD ALWAYS FILE YOUR TAX RETURNS.

DON'T IGNORE NOTICES FROM THE IRS

A letter from the IRS is rarely a good thing. One of the worst missives to get from the tax man is the *1058 Notice* or the *CP90 – Final Notice Before Levy*. It is a final warning shot to scare you into paying up and should NOT be ignored. If either of these land in your mailbox, you have little time to react, so get help quickly! You will receive several letters, about 4 – 5 weeks apart, notifying you that there is a balance due before these bad boys go out. The sooner you respond, the easier it will be for your tax resolution specialist to protect you.

IRS letters are actually legal notices required to be sent prior to commencement of forced collection activities. Taxpayers who are non-responsive end up in forced collections, causing themselves tremendous financial pain. The IRS is the most powerful debt collection agency on the planet. They can take your stuff without a court order. A tax resolution specialist is capable of preventing forced collection activity, but you need to get help from one ASAP.

So, what happens if you ignore the letters and the IRS starts forced collections? The IRS knows they can take your money, assets and/or income. They also intend to collect the most money for the least effort and cost, as they have been left horribly underfunded.

Levies

The IRS usually starts off by going after your bank accounts with a levy. This means they can seize any money you have in the bank. All they need to do is give the bank notice, then wait. They don't have to wait very long either. Once your bank gets the levy notice, they will freeze the account. This means that no money can be taken out of the account until the IRS gets their levy. After 21 days, if you have not contacted the IRS to dispute or pay your tax, they take all the money in the account up to the amount of your unpaid tax balance.

Wage Garnishment

The next source of low-hanging fruit is your paycheck. They will send your employer a garnishment notice. Oftentimes, they take 75% of your net pay and leave you with a mere 25% to pay your bills. Even worse, I have heard of garnishments that leave a taxpayer with only 10% of their take-home pay. The garnishment is a continuous levy, unlike the bank levy which is a one-time deal. This means that every future paycheck you receive will be garnished. Although it's illegal for an employer to fire you for receiving an IRS garnishment, it happens all the time. The employer finds any excuse they can to get rid of you because they fear that the IRS will come by to poke around.

Assets

After taking your money and income, the IRS will go after your assets. To protect the government's interest, they file a federal tax lien against you. This makes borrowing money nearly impossible. While tax liens are no longer reported to the credit bureaus, all tax liens are published quarterly by the IRS. Financial institutions have access to this database, so if your name appears on the list, you will likely be denied for a loan. It may also prevent you from selling your more valuable assets, unless the IRS gets the proceeds.

Let's take a minute to review. In this scenario, you have no money in the bank, you're suffering a 75% cut in take-home pay, you can't sell your stuff, and you can't borrow money. They did all of this without having to take you to court. This is what forced collection looks like.

As I said earlier, the IRS is the most powerful debt collection agency on the planet. But the situation doesn't have to escalate to the extent of the above scenario. Forced collection can be prevented, but only if you properly respond to the notices.

Do you recall what I mentioned in the first paragraph of the book? In case you forgot—there is definitely a solution for you!

3

THE TAXPAYER BILL OF RIGHTS

The Taxpayer Advocate Service (TAS) is an independent organization within the IRS. Their job is to ensure that every taxpayer is treated fairly and that you know and understand your rights. According to the TAS website, www.taxpayeradvocate.irs.gov, they want you to know that you have rights. They are also available to help protect your rights and resolve tax problems you can't solve on your own. Now let me tell you more about what TAS wants you to know.

The IRS has adopted a Taxpayer Bill of Rights as proposed by National Taxpayer Advocate Nina Olson. It applies to all taxpayers in their dealings with the IRS. The Taxpayer Bill of Rights groups the existing rights in the tax code into ten fundamental rights, and makes them clear, understandable, and accessible.

In this section we'll cover the following Bill of Rights and what each means for you:

1. The Right to Be Informed
2. The Right to Pay No More Than the Correct Amount of Tax
3. The Right to Challenge the IRS's Position and Be Heard
4. The Right to Appeal an IRS Decision in an Independent Forum
5. The Right to Finality
6. The Right to Privacy
7. The Right to Confidentiality
8. The Right to Retain Representation
9. The Right to a Fair and Just Tax System

THE RIGHT TO BE INFORMED

Taxpayers have the right to know what they need to do to comply with tax laws. They are entitled to clear explanations of the law and IRS procedures in all tax forms, instructions, publications, notices, and correspondence. Taxpayers have the right to be informed of IRS decisions about their tax accounts and to receive clear explanations of the outcomes.

What This Means for You

- If you receive a notice fully or partially disallowing your refund claim, including a refund you claim on your income tax return, it must explain the specific reasons why the claim is being disallowed. IRC § 6402(l)

- Generally, if you owe a penalty, each written notice of such penalty must provide an explanation of the penalty, including the name of the penalty, the authority under the Internal Revenue Code, and how it is calculated. IRC § 6751(a)

- During an in-person interview with the IRS as part of an audit, the IRS employee must explain the audit process and your rights under that process. Likewise, during an in-person interview with the IRS concerning the collection of your tax, the IRS employee must explain the collection process and your rights under that process. IRC § 7521(b)(1) Generally, the IRS uses *Publication 1, Your Rights as a Taxpayer* to meet this requirement.

- The IRS must include on certain notices the amount (if any) of the tax, interest, and certain penalties you owe and must explain why you owe these amounts. IRC § 7522

- The IRS must inform you in certain publications and instructions that when you file a joint income tax return with your spouse, both of you are responsible for all tax due and any additional amounts due for that tax year, unless "innocent spouse" relief applies. RRA 98 § 3501(a)

- The IRS must inform you in *Publication 1, Your Rights as a Taxpayer* and all collection-related notices that in certain circumstances you may be relieved of all or part of the tax owed with your joint return. This is sometimes referred to as "innocent spouse relief." RRA 98 § 3501(b)

- The IRS must explain in *Publication 1, Your Rights as a Taxpayer* how it selects which taxpayers will be audited. RRA 98 § 3503

- If the IRS proposes to assess tax against you, it will send you a letter providing the examination report, stating the proposed changes, and providing you with the opportunity for a review by an Appeals Officer if you respond (generally) within 30 days. This letter, which in some cases is the first communication from the examiner, must provide an explanation of the entire process from examination (audit) through collection and explain that the Taxpayer Advocate Service may be able to assist you. RRA § 3504 Generally, *Publication 3498, The Examination Process*, or *Publication 3498-A, The Examination Process* (Audits by Mail) is included with this letter.

- If you enter into a payment plan—also known as an installment agreement—the IRS must send you an annual statement that details how much you owed at the beginning of the year, how much you paid during the year, and how much you still owe at the end of the year. RRA § 98 3506, Treas. Reg. § 301.6159-1(h)

- You have the right to access certain IRS records, including instructions and manuals, unless such records are required or permitted to be withheld under the Internal Revenue Code, the Freedom of Information Act, or the Privacy Act. Certain IRS records must be made available to you electronically.

- If the IRS is proposing to adjust the amount of tax you owe, you will typically be sent a statutory notice

of deficiency which informs you of the proposed
change. This notice provides you with a right to
challenge the proposed adjustment in Tax Court
without first paying the proposed adjustment. To
exercise this right, you must file a petition with the
Tax Court within 90 days of the date of the notice
being sent (or 150 days if the taxpayer's address on
the notice is outside the United States or if the
taxpayer is out of the country at the time the notice
is mailed). Thus, the statutory notice of deficiency is
your ticket to Tax Court. IRC §§ 6212; 6213(b)

- The IRS should ensure that its written guidance and
  correspondence is accessible, consistent, easy to
  understand, and written in plain language.

THE RIGHT TO PAY NO MORE THAN THE CORRECT AMOUNT OF TAX

Taxpayers have the right to pay only the amount of tax legally due and to have the IRS apply all tax payments properly.

What This Means for You

- If the IRS is proposing to adjust the amount of tax
  you owe, you will typically be sent a statutory notice
  of deficiency, which informs you of the proposed
  change. This notice provides you with a right to
  challenge the proposed adjustment in Tax Court
  without first paying the proposed adjustment. To
  exercise this right, you must file a petition with the
  Tax Court within 90 days of the date of the notice
  being sent (or 150 days if the taxpayer's address on

the notice is outside the United States or if the taxpayer is out of the country at the time the notice is mailed). Thus, the statutory notice of deficiency is your ticket to Tax Court. IRC §§ 6212; 6213(b)

- If you are an individual taxpayer eligible for Low Income Taxpayer Clinic (LITC) assistance (generally if your income is at or below 250% of the federal poverty level), the IRS may provide information to you about your eligibility for assistance from an LITC. IRC § 7526 For more information, see *IRS Publication 4134, Low Income Taxpayer Clinic List*.

- If you believe you have overpaid your taxes, you can file a refund claim asking for the money back, within certain time limits. IRC § 6402.

See *IRS Publication 17, Your Federal Income Tax* under the heading "What if I Made a Mistake"

See also IRC § 6511: Limitations on claim for credit or refund (statute of limitations) under the Right to Finality.

- You may request that any amount owed be removed if it exceeds the correct amount due under the law, if the IRS has assessed it after the period allowed by law, or if the assessment was done in error or violation of the law. IRC § 6404(a)

See also IRC § 6502: Limitations on collection after assessment (statute of limitations) under the Right to Finality.

- You may request that the IRS remove any interest from your account that was caused by the IRS's unreasonable errors or delays. For example, if the IRS delayed issuing a statutory notice of deficiency because the assigned employee was away for several months attending training, and interest accrued during this time, the IRS may abate the interest as a result of the delay. IRC § 6404(e)

- If you have a legitimate doubt that you owe part or all of the tax debt, you can submit a settlement offer, called an "Offer in Compromise (Doubt as to Liability)" using *Form 656-L*. IRC § 7122

- You will receive an annual notice from the IRS stating the amount of tax due, which will help you check that all payments you made were received by the IRS and correctly applied. IRC § 7524

- If you enter into a payment plan—also known as an installment agreement—the IRS must send you an annual statement that details how much you owed at the beginning of the year, how much you paid during the year, and how much you still owe at the end of the year. RRA § 98 3506, Treas. Reg. § 301.6159-1(h)

THE RIGHT TO CHALLENGE THE IRS'S POSITION AND BE HEARD

Taxpayers have the right to raise objections and provide additional documentation in response to formal IRS actions or proposed actions, to expect that the IRS will consider their timely objections and documentation promptly and fairly, and to receive a response if the IRS does not agree with their position.

What This Means for You

- If you submit documentation or raise objections during an examination, and the IRS does not agree with your position, it will issue a statutory notice of deficiency explaining why it is increasing your tax, which gives you the right to petition the U.S. Tax Court prior to paying the tax. IRC § 6212

- If you are an individual taxpayer eligible for Low Income Taxpayer Clinic (LITC) assistance (generally if your income is at or below 250% of the federal poverty level), the IRS may provide information to you about your eligibility for assistance from an LITC. IRC § 7526

  For more information, see *IRS Publication 4134, Low Income Taxpayer Clinic List.*

- If you are notified by the IRS that it has adjusted your return because of a mathematical or clerical error, you have 60 days to tell the IRS that you disagree. If the IRS is not persuaded, it will issue you a Statutory Notice of Deficiency proposing a tax adjustment. This notice provides you with the right to challenge the proposed adjustment in Tax Court by filing a petition within 90 days of the date of the notice (150 days if the notice is addressed to a person outside the United States), without first paying the proposed adjustment. IRC § 6213(b)

- Immediately after the IRS files a notice of federal tax lien in the appropriate state filing location, the IRS must generally provide you with an opportunity for a hearing before an independent IRS Appeals/Settlement Officer. At that hearing, you can raise alternatives to the IRS's collection action and may even be able to challenge whether you actually owe the tax. If you disagree with Appeals' determination, you can go to Tax Court. IRC § 6320

- Before the IRS takes its first enforcement action to collect a tax debt by levying, for example, your bank account, the IRS must generally provide you with an opportunity for a hearing before an independent IRS Appeals/Settlement Officer. At that hearing, you can raise alternatives to the IRS's collection action and may even be able to challenge whether you actually owe the tax. If you disagree with Appeals' determination, you can go to Tax Court. IRC § 6330

THE RIGHT TO APPEAL AN IRS DECISION IN AN INDEPENDENT FORUM

Taxpayers are entitled to a fair and impartial administrative appeal of most IRS decisions, including many penalties, and have the right to receive a written response regarding the Office of Appeals' decision. Taxpayers generally have the right to take their cases to court.

What This Means for You

- The Commissioner must ensure an independent IRS Office of Appeals that is separate from the IRS

Office that initially reviewed your case. Generally, Appeals cannot discuss a case with the IRS unless you or your representative is given the opportunity to be present. RRA 98 § 1001(a)(4), Rev. Proc. 2012-18

See *IRS Publication 4227, Overview of the Appeals Process.*

- The IRS must ensure that an Appeals Officer is regularly available within each State.

The IRS lacks a permanent appeals presence in 12 states and Puerto Rico, thereby making it difficult for some taxpayers to obtain timely and equitable face-to-face hearings with an Appeals Officer or Settlement Officer in each state.

- If you do not agree with the proposed adjustment as a result of an examination (audit), you have the right to an administrative appeal. Statement of Procedural Rules, 26 C.F.R. § 601.103(b)

- In certain situations, a taxpayer has the opportunity to request a conference with the Office of Appeals. Statement of Procedural Rules, 26 C.F.R. § 601.103(c)(1)

- You have the right to request an independent review conducted by the Office of Appeals prior to the termination of your installment agreement. IRC § 6159(e)

- If the IRS is proposing to adjust the amount of tax you owe, you will typically be sent a statutory notice of deficiency, which informs you of the proposed change. This notice provides you with a right to challenge the proposed adjustment in Tax Court without first paying the proposed adjustment. Thus, the statutory notice of deficiency is your ticket to Tax Court. IRC § 6212

- To exercise your right to challenge the proposed adjustment in Tax Court without first paying the proposed adjustment, you must file a petition with the Tax Court within 90 days of the date of the notice being sent (or 150 days if the taxpayer's address on the notice is outside the United States or if the taxpayer is out of the country at the time the notice is mailed). IRC § 6213

- In certain circumstances, the Office of Appeals has exclusive authority to settle your case. Generally, for the four months after you petition Tax Court, Appeals will be the only office within the IRS who can settle your case, as long as the statutory notice of deficiency or other notice of determination was not issued by Appeals. Statement of Procedural Rules, 26 C.F.R. § 601.106

- Generally, you are entitled to request a Collection Due Process hearing to dispute the first proposed levy action relating to a particular tax liability. The independent IRS Appeals/Settlement Officer conducting your hearing must have no prior involvement with the taxes the IRS is attempting to collect. If you disagree with the hearing officer's determination, you can challenge it in Tax Court. IRC § 6330

- If the IRS rejects your request for an Offer in Compromise asking the IRS to settle your tax debt for less than the amount owed, or a payment plan—also known as an installment agreement—then you may seek an independent review of the rejection with the IRS Office of Appeals. IRC § 6159(f) / IRC § 7122(e).

- You can generally request that an issue you have not been able to resolve with the IRS examination or collection division be transferred to the Office of Appeals. For issues that are unresolved after working with Appeals, you may request non-binding mediation (where a neutral third party will help you try to reach a settlement) or binding arbitration (where you and the IRS will be bound by a third party's decision). You may also request non-binding mediation or arbitration after unsuccessfully trying to enter into a closing agreement or offer in compromise. IRC § 7123

- Generally, if you have fully paid the tax and your tax refund claim is denied or if no action is taken on the claim within six months, then you may file a refund suit in a United States District Court or the United States Court of Federal Claims. IRC § 7422

- In very limited circumstances, you can ask a court to make a determination on certain tax issues prior to there being an actual dispute between you and the IRS. For example, a court may be able to determine whether an organization is tax-exempt or if a retirement plan is valid. IRC §§ 7428, 7476-7479

- A jeopardy levy or assessment allows the IRS, in very limited circumstances, to bypass normal administrative safeguards and protections. For example, the IRS may issue a jeopardy levy if the IRS has knowledge that the taxpayer is fleeing the country. If the IRS makes such a jeopardy levy or assessment, you have the right to file a law suit and the court will determine whether the levy or assessment was reasonable under the circumstances and whether the amount is appropriate. IRC § 7429

THE RIGHT TO FINALITY

Taxpayers have the right to know the maximum amount of time they have to challenge the IRS's position as well as the maximum amount of time the IRS has to audit a particular tax year. Taxpayers have the right to know when the IRS has finished an audit.

What This Means for You

- In order to timely challenge a statutory notice of deficiency in Tax Court, you must file your petition within 90 days of the date of the statutory notice of deficiency, or 150 days if the taxpayer's address on the notice is outside the United States or if the taxpayer is out of the country at the time the notice is mailed. If you do not timely file a petition, the amount proposed in the statutory notice will be assessed and you will receive a bill. IRC § 6213

- If you receive a notice proposing additional tax (statutory notice of deficiency), the notice must include the deadline for filing a petition with the Tax Court to challenge the amount proposed. IRC § 6213(a)

- The IRS generally has three years from the date your return was filed to assess the tax. There are some limited exceptions to the three-year rule, such as not filing a return or filing a fraudulent return. IRC § 6501

- The IRS generally has ten years from the assessment date to collect unpaid taxes from you. However, there are a number of circumstances where the ten year collection period may be suspended, such as during the period when the IRS cannot collect, such as bankruptcy, when a collection due process proceeding, or when an offer in compromise is pending. IRC § 6502

- If you believe you have overpaid your taxes, you can file a refund claim asking for the money back. Generally, you must file a refund claim within three years from the date you filed your original return or two years from the date you paid the tax, whichever is later. IRC § 6511

See also IRC § 6402: Administrative claim for refund under the Right to Pay No More than the correct amount of tax.

- If you or the IRS does not file a timely appeal, the decision of the U.S. Tax Court is final. IRC § 7481

- Generally, you will only be subject to one

examination per taxable year. However, the IRS may reopen a taxable year that has been previously examined if the IRS finds it necessary (e.g., there is evidence of fraud). IRC § 7605(b)

THE RIGHT TO PRIVACY

Taxpayers have the right to expect that any IRS inquiry, examination, or enforcement action will comply with the law and be no more intrusive than necessary, and will respect all due process rights, including search and seizure protections and a collection due process hearing where applicable.

What This Means for You

- During a Collection Due Process hearing, an independent IRS Appeals/Settlement Officer must consider whether the IRS's lien filing balances the government's need for the efficient collection of taxes with your legitimate concern that the IRS's collection actions are no more intrusive than necessary. IRC § 6320

- During a Collection Due Process hearing, an independent IRS Appeals/Settlement Officer must consider whether the IRS's proposed levy action balances the government's need for the efficient collection of taxes with your legitimate concern that the IRS's collection actions are no more intrusive than necessary. IRC § 6330

- The IRS cannot levy any of your personal property in the following situations: before it sends you a notice of demand, while you have a request for a payment plan pending, or if the IRS will not recover any money from seizing and selling your property. IRC § 6331

- The IRS cannot seize certain personal items, such as necessary schoolbooks, clothing, undelivered mail, certain amounts of furniture and household items, and tools of a trade. IRC § 6334(a)

- There are limits on the amount of wages that the IRS can levy (seize) in order to collect tax that you owe. A portion of wages equivalent to the standard deduction combined with any deductions for personal exemptions is protected from levy. IRC § 6334(d)

- The IRS cannot seize your personal residence, including a residence used as a principal residence by your spouse, former spouse, or minor child, without first getting court approval, and it must show there is no reasonable alternative for collecting the tax debt from you. IRC § 6334(e) Treas. Reg. § 301.6334-1(d)(1)

The revenue officer must attempt to personally contact you and if you indicate the seizure would cause a hardship, he or she must assist you in contacting the Taxpayer Advocate Service if not providing the requested relief. IRM 5.10.1.7.2

The IRS issued interim guidance that extends these protections to suits to foreclose a lien on a principal residence. This means that the IRS cannot ask a judge to give them permission to take away your personal residence, putting you out on the street. According to this guidance, the IRS should not pursue a suit to foreclose a lien on your principal residence unless it has considered hardship issues and there are no reasonable administrative remedies. See *IRS Interim Guidance Memo SBSE-05-0414-0032*.

- As soon as practicable after seizure, the IRS must provide written notice to the owner of the property that the property will be put up for sale. Before the sale of the property, the IRS shall determine a minimum bid price. Before the property is sold, if the owner of the property pays the amount of the tax liability plus the expenses associated with the seizure, the IRS will return the property to the owner. Within 180 days after the sale, any person having an interest in the property may redeem the property sold by paying the amount the purchaser paid plus interest. This offers a second chance to keep the property if the owner can arrange to have a family member buy it back. IRC §§ 6335, 6337

- If the IRS sells your property, you will receive a breakdown of how the money received from the sale of your property was applied to your tax debt. IRC § 6340

- Under § 3421 of the Restructuring and Reform Act of 1998, IRS employees are required "where appropriate," to seek approval by a supervisor prior to filing a Notice of Federal Tax Lien. Section 3421 further requires that disciplinary action be taken when such approval is not obtained. RRA § 98 3421

- The IRS should not seek intrusive and extraneous information about your lifestyle during an audit if there is no reasonable indication that you have unreported income. IRC § 7602(e)

- If you submit an offer to settle your tax debt, and the offer relates only to how much you owe (known as a Doubt as to Liability Offer in Compromise), you do not need to submit any financial documentation. IRC § 7122(d)(3)(B)

For information, see Form 656-L, Offer in Compromise (Doubt as to Liability).

THE RIGHT TO CONFIDENTIALITY

Taxpayers have the right to expect that any information they provide to the IRS will not be disclosed, unless authorized by the taxpayer or by law. Taxpayers have the right to expect the IRS to investigate and take appropriate action against its employees, return preparers, and others who wrongfully use or disclose taxpayer return information.

What This Means for You

- In general, the IRS may not disclose your tax information to third parties unless you give it permission, e.g., you request that they disclose information in connection with a mortgage or student loan application. IRC § 6103

- If a tax return preparer discloses or uses your tax information for any purpose other than for tax preparation, the preparer may be subject to civil penalties. If the disclosure or improper use is done knowingly or recklessly, the preparer may also be subject to criminal fines and imprisonment. IRC §§ 6713, 7216

- Communications between you and an attorney with respect to legal advice the attorney gives you are generally privileged. A similar privilege applies to tax advice you receive from an individual who is authorized to practice before the IRS (e.g., certified public accountant, enrolled agent, and enrolled actuary), but only to the extent that the communication between you and that individual would be privileged if it had been between you and an attorney.

  For example, communication between you and an individual who is authorized to practice before the IRS regarding the preparation of a tax return, is not privileged because there would be no similar privilege between a taxpayer and an attorney. The privilege relating to taxpayer communications with an individual authorized to practice before the IRS only applies in the context of noncriminal tax matters before the IRS, and noncriminal tax proceedings in Federal court where the United States is a party. IRC § 7525

- In general, the IRS cannot contact third parties, e.g., your employer, neighbors, or bank, to obtain information about adjusting or collecting your tax liability unless it provides you with reasonable notice in advance. Subject to some exceptions, the IRS is

- required to periodically provide you a list of the third party contacts and upon request. IRC § 7602(c)

- The National Taxpayer Advocate and Local Taxpayer Advocates may decide whether to share with the IRS any information you (or your representative) provide them regarding your tax matter, including the fact that you've contacted the Taxpayer Advocate Service. IRC § 7803(c)(4)(A)(iv)

THE RIGHT TO RETAIN REPRESENTATION

Taxpayers have the right to retain an authorized representative of their choice to represent them in their dealings with the IRS. Taxpayers have the right to be told that if they cannot afford to hire a representative they may be eligible for assistance from a Low Income Taxpayer Clinic.

What This Means for You

- If you have won your case in court, under certain conditions, you may be entitled to recover certain reasonable administrative and litigation costs related to your dispute with the IRS. IRC § 7430

- In most situations, the IRS must suspend an interview if you request to consult with a representative, such as an attorney, Certified Public Accountant (CPA), or Enrolled Agent (EA). IRC § 7521(b)(2)

- You may select a person, such as an attorney, CPA, or

EA to represent you in an interview with the IRS. The IRS cannot require that you attend with your representative, unless it formally summons you to appear. IRC § 7521(c)

- If you are an individual taxpayer eligible for Low Income Taxpayer Clinic (LITC) assistance (generally your income must be at or below 250 percent of the federal poverty level), you may ask an LITC to represent you (for free or a minimal fee) in your tax dispute before the IRS or federal court. IRC § 7526

For more information, see Publication 4134, Low Income Taxpayer Clinic List.

THE RIGHT TO A FAIR AND JUST TAX SYSTEM

Taxpayers have the right to expect the tax system to consider facts and circumstances that might affect their underlying liabilities, ability to pay, or ability to provide information timely. Taxpayers have the right to receive assistance from the Taxpayer Advocate Service if they are experiencing financial difficulty or if the IRS has not resolved their tax issues properly and timely through its normal channels.

What This Means for You

- If you cannot pay your tax debt in full and you meet certain conditions, you can enter into a payment plan with the IRS where you pay a set amount over time, generally on a monthly basis. IRC § 6159

See TAS Toolkit, Installment Agreements.

- You may request that any amount owed be eliminated if it exceeds the correct amount due under the law, if the IRS has assessed it after the period allowed by law, or if the assessment was done in error or violation of the law. IRC § 6404(a)

See also IRC § 6502: Limitations on collection after assessment (statute of limitations) under the Right to Finality

- You may request that the IRS remove any interest from your account that was caused by the IRS's unreasonable errors or delays. For example, if the IRS delays issuing a statutory notice of deficiency because the assigned employee was away for several months attending training, and interest accrues during this time, the IRS may abate the interest as a result of the delay. IRC § 6404(e)

- The time limit for asking for the taxes you paid to be refunded may be suspended during the time you are unable to manage your financial affairs due to a mental or physical health problem. IRC § 6511(h)

- If you have acted with reasonable care, you may be entitled to relief from certain penalties. Additionally, if you have a reasonable basis for taking a particular tax position, such as a position on your return or a claim for refund, you may be entitled to relief from certain penalties. Reliance on the advice of a tax professional can in certain circumstances represent reasonable cause for the abatement of certain penalties. IRC §§ 6651, 6656, 6694, 6662, 6676

- If you use a return preparer who takes an unreasonable or reckless position that results in underreporting your tax, that preparer may be subject to penalties. IRC § 6694

- You can submit an Offer in Compromise asking the IRS to settle your tax debt for less than the full amount if you believe (1) you do not owe all or part of the tax debt, (2) if you are unable to pay all of the tax debt within the time permitted by law to collect, or (3) there are factors such as equity, hardship, or public policy that you think the IRS should consider in determining whether to compromise your liability. IRC § 7122

   See page 289 of the RRA 98 Conference Report, H.R. Rep. No. 105-599 (Conf. Rep.).

- If you have are experiencing a significant hardship because of IRS action or inaction, you may be eligible for assistance from the Taxpayer Advocate Service (TAS). A significant hardship occurs when a tax problem causes you financial difficulties, or if you have been unable to resolve your problem through normal IRS channels. You may also be eligible if you believe an IRS system or procedure isn't working as it should. IRC § 7803(c)

- You have the right to request that the Taxpayer Advocate Service issue a Taxpayer Assistance Order (TAO) on your behalf if you are experiencing a significant hardship. TAS can issue a TAO ordering the IRS to take certain actions, cease certain actions, or refrain from taking certain actions, and it can also order the IRS to reconsider, raise to a higher level, or speed up an action. IRC § 7811

- If you are trying to settle your tax debt with an Offer in Compromise based on your inability to pay, the IRS considers your income, assets, and expenses in deciding whether to accept your offer. Generally, the IRS uses guidelines for standard allowances for cost of living expenses. But, if you will not able to pay your basic living expenses, then the IRS must consider your actual expenses. If you are offering to settle because you believe you don't owe the tax liability, you will not need to submit financial information. IRC § 7122(d)(2)

- If you are a low income taxpayer trying to settle your tax debt with an Offer in Compromise, the IRS cannot reject your offer solely on the basis of the amount offer. For example, it cannot reject an offer solely because the amount offered is so low it does not cover the IRS costs for processing the offer. IRC § 7122(d)(3)(A)

- If you submit an offer to settle your tax debt, and the offer relates only to how much you owe (known as a "Doubt as to Liability Offer in Compromise"), the IRS cannot reject your offer solely because it cannot locate your tax return to verify how much you owe. IRC § 7122(d)(3)(B)

- The IRS cannot levy (seize) all of your wages to collect your unpaid tax. A portion will be exempt from levy to allow you to pay basic living expenses. IRC § 6334

- The IRS must release all or part of a levy and notify the person upon whom the levy was made if one of the following situations exist: 1) the underlying liability is satisfied or becomes unenforceable due to the lapse of time, 2) the taxpayer enters into an installment agreement, unless the agreement specifies otherwise, 3) the release of the levy will facilitate collection of liability, 4) the IRS determines the levy is creating an economic hardship for the taxpayer, or 5) the fair market value of the property levied is greater than the liability and releasing the levy on part of the property would not impair collection of the underlying liability. IRC § 6343(a)(1)

- If you are an individual taxpayer eligible for Low Income Taxpayer Clinic (LITC) assistance (generally your income must be at or below 250 percent of the federal poverty level guidelines), you have the right to seek assistance from an LITC to ensure that your particular facts and circumstances are being considered by the IRS. IRC § 7526

For more information, see *Publication 4134, Low Income Taxpayer Clinic List.*

- If the IRS is proposing to adjust the amount of tax you owe, you will typically be sent a statutory notice of deficiency, which informs you of the proposed change. This notice provides you with a right to challenge the proposed adjustment in Tax Court without first paying the proposed adjustment. To exercise this right, you must file a petition with the Tax Court within 90 days of the date of the notice being sent (or 150 days if the taxpayer's address on the notice is outside the United States or if the taxpayer is out of the country at the time the notice is mailed). Thus, the statutory notice of deficiency is your ticket to Tax Court. IRC §§ 6212; 6213(b)

Now that you're aware of your rights as a taxpayer, be sure to work with someone in a position to protect those rights for you—or at least be in a position to speak up for yourself. This leads perfectly into the next topic of discussion: Should you hire a professional?

4

DO IT YOURSELF OR HIRE A PROFESSIONAL

One of the biggest benefits to hiring a tax professional to represent you before the IRS is that once you do, you aren't required to speak directly to the IRS anymore. That's right—the IRS cannot contact you if you have a legally appointed representative.

POWER OF ATTORNEY

All you need to do is sign *Form 2848*, a limited power of attorney which appoints your chosen professional to represent you before the IRS in the dispute. Once filed, if the IRS tries to contact you again you may respectfully reply "please direct those inquiries to my representative," and they are required to comply. That will be the extent of your personal contact with IRS agents from then on.

Only if your tax dispute is small should you represent yourself. Think about whether you would go to court without a lawyer—probably not. The IRS has no obligation to assure that you receive the best possible resolution allowed by law.

So, unless you know your rights and the law, you may not be your own best advocate.

Taxpayers are always permitted to represent themselves, but if you owe more than $10,000 in taxes or you have income or assets worthy of protecting, consider hiring someone competent to represent you. In some cases, the amount you pay for professional representation actually costs you nothing since the professional fees reduce the amount you pay to the IRS dollar for dollar.

WHO CAN REPRESENT YOU?

There are only three credentialed professionals allowed to represent a taxpayer in an IRS dispute: an Attorney, a Certified Public Accountant (CPA), and an Enrolled Agent (EA). Unenrolled tax return preparers have limited ability to talk to the IRS and can only do so for tax returns that they prepared. They are not allowed to represent taxpayers.

Many of the credentialed professionals mentioned here do not practice in the area of tax representation and therefore are not the best choices to advance your position to the most favorable resolution. For instance, a CPA whose main area of practice is auditing financial statements does not necessarily have experience in taxpayer representation. An attorney who mainly represents clients with workers' compensation cases may not be aware of the different procedures required to practice in tax court. An EA who prepares 300 tax returns per year, who focuses on minimizing tax payments for realtors, may not have experience with IRS representation. These people are excellent at what they do, but they do not have high levels of training nor experience in dealing with IRS representation. Taxpayer representation requires complete knowledge of IRS practices and procedures, which is not the same as knowledge of tax law used to prepare a return.

ADVANCED TAX REPRESENTATION CREDENTIALS

In addition to the licensing of credentialed professionals, there are some specialized certifications that signify concentration on tax problem representation. One is the Certified Tax Resolution Specialist (CTRS) designation awarded by The American Society of Tax Problem Solvers (ASTPS). This designation is awarded after a professional has completed advanced levels of training, passed an extensive exam, and satisfied an experience requirement. Membership in ASTPS and the CTRS designation reflects the professional's commitment to excellence and high standards in taxpayer representation.

Another advanced credential to look for is the National Tax Practice Institute Fellowship (NTPIF). NTPI Fellows must complete a rigorous three-level study program covering all facets of client representation before the IRS. Similar to the CTRS designation, the NTPIF shows that the professional knows how to guide clients through the ambiguous labyrinth of IRS codes, regulation, and agency structure.

While considering which professional to hire, you may want to try to find someone in your local area who you are comfortable talking to, since you will be sharing your private financial business. Here are a few suggested questions to ask your professional before signing the engagement letter:

1. How are you qualified for handling tax resolution cases?
2. Do you have experience handling cases similar to mine?
3. What is your success rate?
4. What happens if the IRS rejects my offer?

You should feel comfortable with the professional's answers to these questions, and you should also feel comfortable talking about your issues with them. The professional should be sincere in their desire to help you solve the problem. If you get an "off" vibe, look for another tax resolution professional.

WHO SHOULD YOU AVOID

You hear and see ads all the time on the radio, the Internet, and the TV from "national" firms promoting their services. Many of these firms have been repeatedly sanctioned by the IRS for their aggressive sales tactics and unrealistic promises. Some have even been shut down. They hire unlicensed "sales professionals" who make aggressive, slick pitches to people who do not understand the actual process of tax resolution. By promising to settle your tax debt for "pennies on the dollar," they dupe you into paying their fees in exchange for them just haphazardly filling out a form using your information. Inevitably, your offer is rejected by the IRS, and afterwards the firm may not even talk to you, hiding behind the excuse that they completed your engagement. Avoid all of this by working with someone local who is licensed and has advanced credentials.

While you are well within your rights to represent yourself, I hope you now realize the benefits of seeking professional help. The complexity of the tax code and IRS procedures, along with the high stakes involved, are simply not worth the risk of making a mistake with the IRS. If you make a mistake or take the wrong action, at minimum you will end up paying too much. And you could even end up facing criminal prosecution. Don't take the chance!

5

RESOLUTION STARTS WITH COMPLIANCE

Once you have engaged a resolution professional and given a limited power of attorney, you can find relief from forced collection. Your representative can contact the IRS and ask for a collection activity hold while working to re-establish compliance. If you want a break from the levies, liens, and garnishments, or you don't care to speak to the IRS anymore, you may find it beneficial to hire someone to represent your interests and protect your rights. This is the fastest way to escape the heat.

HOW TO BE "IN COMPLIANCE"

To be "in compliance" does not mean you have to pay off your full account balance. Mainly, the IRS wants you to file all your required returns and be paying your current tax obligations. If your income is from an employer's paycheck, then this can be as simple as making sure your tax withholdings are proper. You can do this by filling out a *Form W-4* and submitting it to your HR department. If you have a complicated situation like a dual earner household, then ask your tax preparer for help.

Self-employed income earners must have the current year's estimated quarterly tax payments all paid. This sometimes requires a bit of strategy if it's late in the year and you don't have enough cash to pay multiple quarterly estimates. One strategy I use with my clients is to get the taxpayer to start depositing tax payments every time income is received. I do this by printing out a stack of estimate payment vouchers for the client, then have them send in a 10 to 20 percent payment each time revenue is collected. You don't necessarily have to wait until the end of the quarter. The IRS will take the money anytime you want to send it! Then by the time the end of the quarter comes, the tax due is already paid.

CATCHING UP THE UNFILED RETURNS

If you have multiple unfiled returns and still have the original records required to prepare those returns, then you are part of the 1% exception. Generally, tax resolution clients need to have the records recreated. This is typically the most onerous phase of the resolution case. As time passes, our memories fade and records disappear.

Luckily, many of your records are quite accessible from the IRS. You can obtain a transcript from the IRS that shows every source of income that has been reported to you. This transcript is called the "wage and income transcript." It shows all your income from W-2s and 1099s, plus some common deductible expense amounts, like student loan interest paid, mortgage interest paid, IRA contributions, health savings account contributions, college tuition payments, and many others. You see, everything that has been reported to the IRS with your social security number or ITIN is kept for up to 10 years. Just ask the IRS for the information and within about a week, you'll receive it in the mail.

The IRS wage and income transcript gets most of the information, but not everything. For instance, business-related expense is not something they have a record of, so you'll need to look through your bank and credit card statements. Most financial institutions have this information available for download directly from your online account. They may have older records available by request if you cannot obtain enough history online.

USING ESTIMATES

Even if you have no way to recreate the expense records, a tax return can be filed using estimates. There are publications that use survey data to list average expense percentages for nearly every business or occupation. CCH Publication's "Almanac of Business & Industrial Financial Ratios" is an excellent resource. If you have the income portion of your tax return figured out, then use the estimate percentages to fill in the expense portion and you will have satisfied the filing requirement. In the tax return, you will need to disclose why estimates are used instead of actual records, and you will also need to identify the source of estimate data.

CASE STUDY EXAMPLE #1

> Consider this case example of how a tax problem can be resolved by properly filing accurate past tax returns: The taxpayer had four years of unfiled returns and started receiving threatening letters from the IRS. In

this case, the IRS filed substitute returns for the taxpayer. If a taxpayer fails to file a return, the IRS has the authority to file a return on the taxpayer's behalf, but the IRS is *not* required to give the benefit of any expense deductions. The taxpayer was assessed $62,000 of tax, penalties, and interest. After the accurate original returns were filed, the balance was reduced to $3,800. The taxpayer happily paid off the balance and moved on with his life. Sometimes it really is just that simple.

6

STATUTE OF LIMITATIONS

The IRS has a time limit to take certain actions when it comes to your taxes. This time limit is commonly referred to as the "statute of limitations." If they fail to act within the statutorily prescribed timeframe, their actions are not legal and therefore prohibited. These time limits are established by the Internal Revenue Code. The time limit applies to the taxpayer as well, with concern to claims for refunds of overpayments. So, sometimes the statute of limitations works for you, and other times it works against you. I will give an overview of the three statute of limitations of greatest concern to the taxpayer, without getting into the calculation details. Calculation of statute expiration dates can be quite complicated!

ASSESSMENT STATUTE EXPIRATION DATE (ASED)

The ASED refers to the amount of time that the IRS is allowed to assess taxes. Taxes must be assessed within three years from the date the return is filed or due, whichever is later. If the IRS fails to assess a tax within this three year limit, they cannot assess or collect the tax.

If a tax return contains a substantial understatement of gross income, the statute of limitations is extended by an additional three years. The IRS defines substantial understatement as 25% or more of the gross income. That means that if the return has a 25% understatement of gross income, then the assessment statute is extended from three years to six years.

The assessment statute is unlimited for the following cases, meaning the IRS can take as long as it wants to collect the tax:

- Unfiled return or Unsigned Substitute for Return (SFR)
- Filing a false or fraudulent return with the intent to evade tax
- An attempt is made to defeat or evade the tax
- A properly filed amended return filed after a fraudulently filed return does NOT limit the statute of limitations

In case you missed it, an unfiled return does not have a statute of limitations. So always FILE THE RETURN!

COLLECTION STATUTE EXPIRATION DATE

Once you're assessed the tax, the IRS then has 10 years from the assessment date to collect the tax. If you are lucky enough to make it through 10 years of collection action, or they just don't get around to your case, then you are done. You don't have to pay the tax. By law, the IRS is barred from taking any further action against you. In some special cases, this is a viable resolution strategy. You just wait it out by stalling collection action.

If you are going to use the "wait it out" strategy, then it is imperative you know what actions can pause the running of the statute clock. Actions that pause the clock are also known as "tolling events."

The idea here is to be fair to the IRS. It prevents people from taking actions to prevent collection activity, that then steal away time from the IRS in terms of their stature. For instance, filing for bankruptcy causes an Automatic Stay that prevents creditors, including the IRS, from collecting money from the individual. If not for the tolling event, someone could file for bankruptcy just as the statute time was running out, not intending to go through with the bankruptcy, but using the Automatic Stay to prevent IRS from taking action. This would essentially shorten the CSED. Consequently, the duration of the Automatic Stay plus 6 months is added to the CSED, thereby preventing such tactics. Besides bankruptcy, a few other tolling events are:

- Certain appeal requests
- Filing a lawsuit against the IRS
- A 6-month absence from the country
- Submitting an Offer in Compromise
- Requesting an Installment Agreement
- Filing an Innocent Spouse defense

Tolling events are just one of the factors that complicate calculating accurate statute of limitation expiration dates. Often, the IRS's calculations of these dates are in error, so prudent practice is to review the ASED and CSED to see if the IRS is barred by the law from assessing or collecting the tax in dispute.

REFUND STATUTE EXPIRATION DATE

This is the one which works against the taxpayer, especially if you failed to file a tax return. Remember... always FILE THE RETURN.

Here's the reason why. The statute of limitations gives three years from the date the return was filed or two years from the date that the tax was paid to properly make a claim for a refund. If you fail to file a return, then you only have two years from the date that the tax was paid to claim your refund, otherwise the IRS gets to keep your overpayment. OUCH!

The point of this chapter was to make you aware that there are specific time limits within which to act, otherwise the action is prohibited. The statute expiration dates discussed are best calculated by a professional. It is also important to consider these expiration dates in conjunction with an overall strategy for resolution. It may be in your best interest to avoid pausing the clock and just waiting it out, but that determination is for your tax resolution specialist to make.

7

CURRENTLY NON-COLLECTABLE

Suppose you owe the IRS and cannot afford to pay anything. If your income is limited and you're finding it difficult to meet your current living expenses and you have little equity in assets (you can't sell your things for much more than you owe on them), then you can ask to be left alone. The IRS understands that if you absolutely cannot pay them, then it makes little sense to badger you for money. If this describes your current circumstance, you qualify to be placed in Currently Non-Collectable status (CNC).

Once you are granted CNC status, the IRS stops all collection activity. The good news is that you are left alone for a while, but penalty and interest charges continue to accrue. That means your balance owed grows each day. Most people who qualify for CNC seldom care about that as long as they don't have to worry about getting wages garnished and bank accounts seized. This is only temporary though; the IRS reviews CNC status taxpayers periodically to be sure they still qualify.

COLLECTION STATUTE EXPIRATION DATE

There is one more benefit to CNC status that's worth mentioning. While in CNC status, the collection statute expiration date (CSED) clock continues to run. If you are able to remain in CNC status until the statute of limitations prohibits action, you may be able to walk away from the entire debt. For taxpayers who have fallen upon hard times, CNC status is an oasis of relief.

CASE STUDY EXAMPLE #2

> As an example, here is one of my clients' CNC cases: A self-employed taxpayer's industry was in recession and work was scarce. The taxpayer had failed to make estimated tax payments and owed over $12,000 after filing his tax return. He has no ability to pay and minimal equity in assets. He began receiving collection letters, which caused him high levels of anxiety. We were able to negotiate that the client be placed in CNC status to stop the collection activity. The letters stopped and the client was relieved from the burden of the tax bill as long as the current financial situation persisted. This allowed the taxpayer opportunity to find work without the added pressure of IRS collections.

8

PENALTY AND INTEREST ABATEMENT

According to the IRS's Internal Revenue Manual, taxpayers in the United States assess their tax liabilities against themselves and pay them voluntarily. This system of self-assessment and payment is based on the principle of voluntary compliance. Voluntary compliance exists when taxpayers conform to the law without compulsion or threat.

Compliant self-assessment requires a taxpayer to know the rules for filing returns and paying taxes. The IRS is responsible for providing information to taxpayers, which includes the following:

- Written materials that clearly explain the rules, and
- Forms that permit the self-computation of tax liability.

In addition, the IRS must also provide a means to preserve and enhance our voluntary compliance by fairly, consistently, and accurately administering a system of penalties.

Although penalties support and encourage voluntary compliance, they also serve to bring additional revenue into the Treasury and to indirectly fund enforcement costs. However, collecting additional funding is not the reason for creating or imposing penalties. Penalties advance the mission of the IRS when they encourage voluntary compliance. The IRS has formalized this obligation to the public in its mission statement: "Provide America's taxpayers top quality service by helping them understand and meet their tax responsibilities and enforce the law with integrity and fairness to all."

Voluntary compliance is achieved when a taxpayer makes a good faith effort to meet the tax obligations defined by the Internal Revenue Code.

Penalties support voluntary compliance by assuring compliant taxpayers that tax offenders are identified and penalized.

Since the IRS has the obligation to advance the fairness and effectiveness of the tax system, penalties should do the following:

- Be severe enough to deter noncompliance,
- Encourage noncompliant taxpayers to comply,
- Be objectively proportioned to the offense, and
- Be used as an opportunity to educate taxpayers and encourage their future compliance.

The primary objective of penalties as shown above is to encourage compliance, deter noncompliance, and educate taxpayers. Consequently, when a penalty is assessed and does not accomplish this objective, it may be proper to ask the IRS to abate the penalty. Under certain circumstances, the IRS will grant abatement requests and remove penalties and the interest on those penalties.

One way to minimize the amount of money you must pay the IRS is to ask for interest and penalty abatement. It is often the case that I save a client more than my retainer fee in abatements alone.

INTEREST ABATEMENT

There are very few circumstances under which you can successfully abate interest:

1. The IRS assessed interest on an amount you didn't actually owe.
2. The IRS issued a refund to you erroneously and is seeking to recover the refund plus interest.
3. There was interest charged to you during a time of delay caused by a managerial or ministerial act of the IRS.
4. The IRS failed to notify you of a tax that was due and subsequently charged interest on that amount due.
5. There was interest charged on a tax return which was filed late because you lived in a federally declared disaster area.

In reality, interest abatements are not commonplace, but there are opportunities to ask for them if the right circumstances apply. More often, I get taxpayers' balances reduced by asking for penalty abatement. The IRS does not just comply with any request for abatement though. There are qualifications that must be met for the request to be successful, which we'll now go over.

PENALTY ABATEMENT

There are more than 100 different types of penalties that you can be assessed with. For tax resolution clients, the most common ones are:

1. Failure to file penalty
2. Failure to pay penalty
3. Failure to deposit penalty

These penalties often add up to nearly 50% of the tax amount due. In the case of failure to deposit payroll tax, a responsible party can be assessed penalties of up to 100%. If you are assessed interest compounded daily on this kind of penalty, you can easily see how a penalty abatement could tremendously reduce your liability.

If the taxpayer has reasonable cause for failing to file or pay tax when due and the cause was not due to willful neglect, then the IRS will consider abating the penalty. A reasonable cause for failure to pay is if the payment of the tax would cause undue financial hardship on the taxpayer. But lack of funds in and of itself is not reasonable cause, unless caused by unforeseen or unusual circumstances. One example of this is if the money was used to pay for necessary medical expenses that would otherwise have been foregone if the taxes been paid.

The Internal Revenue Manual (IRM) states that if a taxpayer exercised ordinary business care and prudence but was unable to comply with the law, then penalty abatement may be warranted. A more specific discussion provided by the IRM is as follows, including how to determine if reasonable cause exists.

Ordinary business care and prudence includes making provisions for business obligations to be met when reasonably foreseeable events occur. A taxpayer may establish reasonable cause by providing facts and circumstances showing that he or she exercised ordinary business care and prudence (taking that degree of care that a reasonably prudent person would exercise), but nevertheless were unable to comply with the law.

In determining if the taxpayer exercised ordinary business care and prudence, the following information should be reviewed:

Taxpayer's Reason: The taxpayer's reason should address the penalty imposed. To show reasonable cause, the dates and explanations should clearly correspond with events on which the penalties are based.

Compliance History: Check the preceding tax years (at least three) for payment patterns and the taxpayer's overall compliance history. The same penalty, previously assessed or abated, may indicate that the taxpayer is not exercising ordinary business care. If this is the taxpayer's first incident of noncompliant behavior, this factor can be weighed in with other reasons the taxpayer gives for reasonable cause, since a first time failure to comply does not by itself establish reasonable cause.

Length of Time: Consider the length of time between the event cited as a reason for the noncompliance and subsequent compliance. What should be considered: (1) when the act was required by law, (2) the period of time during which the taxpayer was unable to comply with the law due to circumstances beyond the taxpayer's control, and (3) when the taxpayer complied with the law.

Circumstances Beyond the Taxpayer's Control: Consider whether or not the taxpayer could have anticipated the event that caused the noncompliance. Reasonable cause is generally established when the taxpayer exercises ordinary business care and prudence, but due to circumstances beyond the taxpayer's control, the taxpayer was unable to timely meet the tax obligation. The taxpayer's obligation to meet the tax law requirements is ongoing. Ordinary business care and prudence requires that the taxpayer continue to attempt to meet the requirements, even if late.

Some of the reasonable cause arguments that the IRS considers include:

1. Death, serious illness, or unavoidable absence
2. Fire, casualty, natural disaster, or other disturbance
3. Inability to obtain records
4. A mistake was made
5. Erroneous advice
6. Ignorance of the law
7. Lack of funds despite ordinary business care and prudence
8. Undue economic hardship
9. Taxpayer meets First Time Abatement criteria

The First Time Abatement is worth more discussion here. If you have generally been compliant with filing and paying your taxes on time, you may be a good candidate for a first time penalty abatement. If you meet the following criteria, the IRS will abate penalties for one tax period:

1. You did not have a failure to file or failure to pay penalty assessed in the prior three tax years.

2. You have filed all of your returns and paid or arranged to pay any outstanding tax debt.
3. You did not receive a first time penalty abatement in the last three years.

Even if you do not qualify for a reasonable cause abatement, you can still get a first time penalty abatement as long as you meet the qualifying criteria. You don't even have to provide documentation and you may even be able to get one over the phone.

All of the other reasonable cause penalty abatement requests must be made in writing to the proper IRS campus and be supported by documentation. For your abatement request to have its most favorable chance for success, consider getting help from an experienced professional. Writing a successful penalty abatement request is a science. If you qualify for any of these programs, the professional can typically save you more than the cost of the retainer fee on a penalty abatement request alone.

CASE STUDY EXAMPLE #3

> The taxpayer was assessed a civil penalty for late filing of information returns (1099s). The accountant who she originally hired did not meet the filing deadline, and consequently the taxpayer was forced to hire a different accountant. The second practitioner did get the returns filed, albeit after the filing deadline.
>
> The IRS assessed a penalty of over $15,000 and began sending collection notices to the taxpayer. We prepared a request for abatement due to reasonable cause, which

was reliance on a tax practitioner. We showed that despite the taxpayer's ordinary care and prudence, the information returns were filed late. The taxpayer had an excellent record of filing on time and the period of time that the information returns were late was insignificant. The abatement request was granted, saving the taxpayer over $15,000 in penalties.

9

BANKRUPTCY

Bankruptcy is an influential instrument for resolving your tax debt. If your tax debt qualifies to be discharged, a bankruptcy may be your most favorable and least expensive solution. It can also be used as leverage in negotiation. A threat of filing bankruptcy may help convince the IRS to concede to the taxpayer's position. If you do not qualify for the other programs, or even if you do, consider this as an option.

Bankruptcy is a process of federal court, the purpose of which is to help consumers and businesses eliminate their debts or repay them under the protection of the court. It wipes out most unsecured debt like credit cards and may also save your home from foreclosure.

To discharge your tax debts in bankruptcy, the debts must qualify by meeting some specific criteria. First, the debt must be for income tax. Second, It must have been due for at least three years, including extensions, and must have been assessed for at least 240 days. Third, the tax return must have been filed for at least two years before the filing of the bankruptcy (here is another great reason to always file a tax return!). Fraudulently filed returns or attempts to evade the tax will automatically disqualify the tax debt from bankruptcy relief.

There are different types of bankruptcy cases referred to by the chapters of the bankruptcy code that created them:

- Chapter 7 – The Liquidation Bankruptcy
- Chapter 13 – The Rehabilitation Bankruptcy
- Chapter 11 – The Reorganization Bankruptcy

CHAPTER 7 BANKRUPTCY

This is the type of bankruptcy that involves a trustee who is appointed by the court to take your stuff, sell it at auction, and give the proceeds to your creditors. Afterwards, the creditors have no claim on any of your assets or income, so you go your separate ways. Most people don't lose anything when they file for Chapter 7 bankruptcy because it is common for them to be "upside down" on their loans. In fact, many state statutes provide for exemptions that protect some of your assets from seizure.

The most important benefit of Chapter 7 bankruptcy is the "Automatic Stay." This is often the main reason for filing Chapter 7, because the Automatic Stay prevents creditors from harassing or doing other bad things to the person filing for bankruptcy. The Automatic Stay applies to the IRS as well, so once you file they must cease forced collection activities like garnishments or levies.

At the end of your case, any debts that are discharged become permanently eliminated, including tax debt if it qualifies. If the tax debt does not qualify, then you have the options mentioned earlier as possible solutions.

CHAPTER 13 BANKRUPTCY

The official name of Chapter 13 bankruptcy is the "Adjustment of Debt of an Individual with Regular Income." Under this type of bankruptcy, you generally keep all of your stuff, but you must pay at least some of your outstanding debts. The debt payments typically last three to five years. During this time, you make monthly payments to the Chapter 13 trustee, who then pays it out to your creditors (including the tax debt amounts) according to the "Chapter 13 Plan."

The monthly payments are all of your disposable income. While you get to keep your assets, the bankruptcy court and trustee keep a constant vigil over your financial affairs and expect you to maintain a frugal lifestyle. Once you successfully complete the payments pursuant to the plan, the bankruptcy court discharges the remaining debts. This allows you to start a new financial life current with your obligations.

CHAPTER 11 BANKRUPTCY

If you don't want to file or if you don't qualify for either Chapter 7 or 13 bankruptcy, Chapter 11 may be the solution. This type of bankruptcy is a reorganization typically used with large debts and assets. It is similar to a Chapter 13 case, but the rules are more onerous and complex. This will require a skilled bankruptcy attorney.

Advantages of Chapter 11 Bankruptcy

1. The Automatic Stay protects you from collection activities.
2. You get to keep you assets.
3. You repay all of your unsecured debt at a small percentage of what is owed, spread out over the life of the plan.
4. You can pay non-dischargeable tax debt over the life of the plan without penalty or interest.

Disadvantages of Chapter 11 Bankruptcy

1. You must provide detailed financial statements that become public record.
2. The statute of limitations on your remaining tax debt is suspended from running during the bankruptcy, plus 6 months afterward.
3. The attorney fees for a Chapter 11 bankruptcy are exorbitantly higher than for a Chapter 13.

Bankruptcy is a useful tool for discharging debt (including tax debts) in the hands of a skilled attorney. Additionally, the Automatic Stay will protect you from IRS and other creditors while you are rebuilding your financial life without harassment and forced collection activity. This chapter on bankruptcy was written with the intention of offering an awareness level of information. You must be advised by a bankruptcy attorney to discover the appropriate solution to your specific situation.

10

OFFER IN COMPROMISE

The Offer in Compromise (OIC) program is the well-known program advertised on the radio by national firms who claim to be able to settle your tax debt for pennies on the dollar. But what they fail to mention is that you must meet specific criteria to qualify for the program. The unscrupulous of these big firms make promises that they can eliminate your tax debt, then charge you a large fee to fill out some paperwork, without first evaluating whether you qualify for the program. Once your case is rejected by IRS, they drop you, claiming that the engagement you hired them for is over. The cases of the victims would never have qualified to be presented to the IRS. Be aware of how the Offer in Compromise program works so you don't fall prey to a scam.

That being said, I have seen taxpayers get out of thousands of dollars of tax liabilities with this program, so it is a viable option to settle your tax debt. The OIC is a written agreement between the IRS and a taxpayer, which allows the taxpayer to fully satisfy an unpaid tax liability including interest and penalties for less than the full amount owed. For the taxpayer who qualifies, this program is an escape from an otherwise devastating financial situation.

The Internal Revenue Code gives the IRS the authority to compromise taxes when there is a legitimate dispute of the tax owed (Doubt as to Liability), when it is unlikely that the tax can be collected in full (Doubt as to Collectability), or to promote effective tax administration. This chapter will discuss the most common of the three, the Doubt as to Collectability offer.

The goal of the Doubt as to Collectability (DATC) program is to reach a compromise that is in the best interest of both the taxpayer and the IRS. The IRS gets to collect an amount which it otherwise may not be able to collect, and the taxpayer has an opportunity to settle a dispute and move forward with a fresh start towards voluntary compliance.

You can find an OIC pre-qualifier tool at www.irs.gov to use for a preliminary determination of whether you qualify for the program. The pre-qualifier tool is just for obtaining a preliminary determination of whether you may qualify. It does not give an official decision. The final determination is ultimately made after the IRS reviews a properly submitted application.

DATC ADVANTAGES

The obvious benefit of the Doubt as to Collectability program is that you can completely and permanently settle your tax debt for less than the full amount of the liability. There are some other benefits to the program as well. Unlike a bankruptcy, the OIC does not damage your credit. And once the OIC is accepted and the settlement is paid, the IRS will release the lien filed against you. Afterwards, you can apply for a withdrawal of the federal tax lien, which removes the lien from your public record completely, so it's like the lien was never there. If protecting your ability to obtain credit is a concern, then the OIC is a beneficial resolution option.

DATC DISADVANTAGES

There are also a number of disadvantages to the program. For starters, you must agree to suspend the statute of limitations on assessment for the tax periods covered by the OIC. This allows the IRS more time to assess additional tax for the time that the offer is pending, plus an additional year if the offer is rejected, returned, or terminated. While you do have the right to waive this extension of time, if you do so the IRS may not consider the offer.

In addition to the extended assessment statute of limitations, you also must agree to extend the collection statute of limitations for the time that the offer is pending plus an additional 30 days. The collection statute is also extended by the time an offer is being considered under an appeal. The offer is also contingent upon the taxpayer remaining compliant with filing and paying taxes when due for the next five years. This may seem inconsequential since this is a legal requirement anyway, but it is sometimes difficult for taxpayers who have been continually delinquent, to suddenly fully comply with legal requirements. Having a qualified tax professional's guidance is often imperative to remain compliant. Finally if the offer requires periodic payments over 24 months, the IRS can reinstate the full balance for default of a required payment.

OIC QUALIFICATIONS

To qualify for a Doubt as to Collectability case, the taxpayer must be unable to pay the full amount due through equity in assets and income by the collection statute expiration date. The taxpayer must also be current with all return filing requirements and payments for the most recent year. The offer must be at least what the IRS can otherwise reasonably collect through administrative means. This figure is referred to as the taxpayer's Reasonable Collection Potential (RCP). Determining the validity of this qualification requires a detailed examination of the taxpayer's assets, income, and expenses by an IRS offer examiner. Furthermore, if an offer is submitted for less than the RCP calculation, there must be special circumstances to justify the lower offer, which must be explained in detail to the offer examiner.

The RCP Components: Equity and Income

Without going into full detail of the calculation, let's go over its two main components: the equity component, and the income component. The equity component is calculated by estimating what the proceeds would be if all of the taxpayer's assets were sold, and then all of the loans secured by those assets were paid off. The income component is determined by what the taxpayer's take home pay is, minus allowable expenses. Allowable expenses are what the government deems to be appropriate to support the health and welfare of the taxpayer's family. It is not necessarily what the taxpayer actually spends per month. Basically, if an expense is necessary for the production of income, or the health and welfare of the family, then it is allowed.

Working with a professional who is familiar with what the

IRS will allow is beneficial here. The most effective resolution specialists perform pre-offer submission planning to implement strategies which position the taxpayer in the most favorable position for offer acceptance. In addition, the practitioner can advocate for a taxpayer to allow an expense by showing that it is related to the production of income or is for the support of the family's health and welfare. Often the experienced professional can reduce this component to zero with a bit of planning.

For example, if you drive an old clunker because it is paid off, you may consider upgrading to something newer even if it means paying a note. The new note amount will reduce your offer amount considerably. The amount of the note payments reduce the offer amount, which essentially gets the taxpayer a new car without impacting monthly cash flow. A reliable vehicle is easily justified as required for the production of income.

You can also consider buying health, life, or disability insurance if you have none. Again, the payment you make to the insurance company will reduce your offer amount.

There is even a way for a taxpayer to pay for the tax resolution professional's representation retainer and get a dollar for dollar decrease in the OIC amount, meaning that the IRS pays your professional representation. Can you sense that I'm suggesting you hire a pro to represent you?

I'm keenly aware of the fact that you will get a much better resolution of your tax problem if you hire someone who does this for a living and genuinely cares about helping you. Remember, the IRS is under no obligation to help you find the best resolution. Unless you are well-versed in the Internal Revenue Code or the IRS's Internal Revenue Manual, consider hiring someone who is.

There are two ways to pay for your offer once it has been accepted: the cash payment (or lump sum option), and the monthly periodic payment option. There are advantages and disadvantages to both. Let's take a look at both so you can understand the difference.

LUMP SUM OFFER IN COMPROMISE

An offer is considered lump sum if the amount of the offer will be paid in 5 months or less from the time it is accepted. The IRS will accept a lower dollar amount as an offer if the taxpayer is in a position to pay the offer amount in 5 months or less. The downside to the lump sum offer is that a 20% payment must accompany the offer when it is submitted. If the offer is later rejected, the IRS keeps the 20% payment and applies it to the taxpayer's outstanding balance. If this occurs, you can still appeal the decision but the money will not be returned.

For those interested, I have a strategy to avoid sending in the 20% down payment with the lump sum offer that works like a charm. I would be glad to share it with you if you contact my office.

PERIODIC PAYMENT OFFER IN COMPROMISE

An offer that is to be paid in 6 to 24 months is referred to as a "periodic payment offer in compromise." 24 months is the maximum timeframe allowed to spread the offer payments over. This type of offer requires the 1st payment to be submitted with the offer, rather than the full 20% down payment required by the lump sum offer. In addition, while the offer is under review, the taxpayer must continue to make the monthly periodic payments as shown in the offer. Again, if the offer is rejected, the money is kept and applied to the tax debt.

While this type of offer requires a higher dollar amount offered, it allows a more flexible payment arrangement.

CASE STUDY EXAMPLE #4

> A self-employed contractor owed the IRS over $112,000 due to economic industry fluctuations. As a result, he wasn't able to keep current on his quarterly estimated tax payments for a couple of years. The IRS was also levying his bank account and his 1099 income.
>
> The taxpayer had minimal equity in assets and we did some "financial planning in reverse" so that the taxpayer was positioned as a very good OIC candidate. We obtained levy releases on all income sources and prepared, submitted, and negotiated the offer, and were able to settle the case in full for $11,000, thereby saving our client over $100,000 and having the federal tax liens released! The client got his life back!

FINAL THOUGHTS ON OICS

Due to the fact that an Offer in Compromise can significantly reduce your tax debt, this is where the resolution industry has seen most of the unscrupulous practices. A slick-talking salesperson who has no actual knowledge of the program can easily dupe unsuspecting taxpayers out of substantial fees without first verifying if they qualify for the program. Some national firms have been shut down because of this type of abusive sales tactic.

Work with someone you know or a specialist local to your area who is licensed, like a CPA, EA, or attorney. An ethical practitioner will take the time to get to know you and collect all the facts, then fully evaluate your case and prescribe the most advantageous resolution strategy for you. When it comes to tax resolution firms, bigger is NOT better.

11

INSTALLMENT AGREEMENTS

Many taxpayers do not qualify for the OIC program. For them, the next best way to resolve the money owed to IRS is to pay it back monthly over time. The IRS is statutorily authorized to enter into a written installment agreement which enables a taxpayer to pay the tax liability over a period of time if the arrangement will facilitate the collection of the tax.

To determine if the installment agreement is applicable, the IRS may require the taxpayer to fully disclose income, expense, asset, and liability information. If your balance is below a threshold amount and you will be fully paying the amount due, you will not be required to submit financial information. In certain circumstances, it is important to protect the taxpayer's privacy. In these situations, I suggest that the liability be paid down to below the threshold to avoid the financial disclosure.

I know what you're thinking—if the IRS wanted to find out all about your income and assets, they have the wherewithal to get the information. Nonetheless, you don't have to deliver it to them on a silver platter. Just by making it more difficult for them is sometimes a sufficient deterrent to keep them in the dark.

Now we'll go over the four different kinds of installment agreements available. The differentiating factors are the amount of tax, penalties, and interest assessed.

GUARANTEED INSTALLMENT AGREEMENT

- For taxpayers with less than $10,000 in tax deficiencies (excluding penalties and interest), which can be paid fully within 36 months

Have you heard the radio ads saying that if you owe more than $10,000 they can help settle your tax debt? Did you ever wonder why the $10,000 qualifier is mentioned? I believe they don't want people who owe less than $10,000 because these cases can be resolved through a Guaranteed Installment Agreement.

Here's how it works. If you owe less than $10,000 in tax and can fully pay this amount in 36 months or less, then you will get approved for the Guaranteed Installment Agreement. Acceptance is guaranteed if you meet the qualifications. There are a few more qualifiers though; for the prior five years, you must have been compliant with filing and paying requirements. You also have to agree to remain compliant with filing and payment during the term of the agreement.

According to the *PPC Guide to Dealing With IRS*, taxpayers have a statutory right to an installment agreement. Let's look at the terms required for qualification:

1006.16 IRC Sec. 6159(c) requires the IRS to enter into an installment agreement with the taxpayer if—

- The income tax liability is $10,000 or less, excluding penalties and interest (unlike the criteria for Streamlined Agreements, the dollar limit for Guaranteed Installment Agreements of $10,000 applies to tax only);
- Within the previous five years, the taxpayer has not failed to file or to pay, nor entered into an installment agreement under this provision;
- The installment agreement provides for full payment of the liability within three years;
- The taxpayer agrees to continue to comply with the tax laws and the terms of the agreement for the period (up to three years) that the agreement is in place; and
- If requested by the IRS, the taxpayer submits financial statements, and the IRS determines that the taxpayer is unable to pay the tax due in full. (As a matter of policy, the IRS grants Guaranteed Installment Agreements even if the taxpayer is able to fully pay their accounts.)

These are easy to apply for. At my firm, we offer instructions to taxpayers who qualify for no cost. With a bit of guidance, you can get into one on your own. And I'd like to point out again that the $10,000 threshold applies to TAX AMOUNT only. The balance with penalties and interest can actually be more than $10,000 and still qualify.

STREAMLINED INSTALLMENT AGREEMENT

- For taxpayers with less than $50,000 in tax deficiencies, penalties, and interest, which can be paid within 72 months or the remaining collection statute of limitations

The Streamlined Installment Agreement can be obtained with limited financial disclosure if the balance is lower than $50,000 and can be fully paid in lesser of 72 months or the remaining collection statute of limitations. In this case, the $50,000 threshold applies to the unpaid balance of assessment (UBA) amount and includes tax, penalties, and interest. The taxpayer is allowed to pay down the due balance to below the threshold amount to qualify.

Due to work backlog, the IRS has increased the threshold limit of the streamlined agreement to $100,000 and the term to 84 months or the remaining collection statute of limitations. This program is ending September 30, 2018 (unless extended). No consideration will be given to the six-year rule (72 months) unless the taxpayer can pay the balance in full by selling assets.

As of late October 2018, there has not yet been an extension granted.

The taxpayer needs to understand that while in the installment agreement, penalties and interest continue to accrue. But if the agreement is properly structured, penalties will be cut in half.

PARTIAL PAYMENT INSTALLMENT AGREEMENT

- Eligibility determined by a full financial disclosure

The Partial Payment Installment Agreement is similar to the Streamlined Installment Agreement, with the exception that it does not pay the balance off in full and requires a full financial disclosure to determine eligibility. This agreement is similar to an Offer in Compromise in that it fully settles the debt for a lesser amount. If full payment is not possible by the collection statute expiration, but the taxpayer has some ability to pay, then the IRS may accept a Partial Payment Installment Agreement.

CASE STUDY EXAMPLE #5

The taxpayer owed $46,000 and was unable to pay it. He contacted the IRS to arrange a monthly payment and was told that his payment would be $800 per month. To encourage payment, the IRS threatened forced collection activity and filed a notice of federal tax lien. Forced collection is when the IRS seizes money from your bank account and/or garnishes your paycheck, other income sources, and state tax refund.

Under a properly structured Partial Payment Installment Agreement, we were able to reduce the monthly payments to $200 over a term of 43 months. We stopped the forced collection threat and had the notice of federal tax lien released. The client settled the debt in total for $8,600 and got to pay it over 43 months. The client received immediate relief and got his life back.

The Partial Payment Installment Agreement is sometimes a more favorable option than an offer in compromise because of the longer payment term.

REGULAR INSTALLMENT AGREEMENT

- Eligibility determined by a full financial disclosure

If none of the previous installment agreements apply to you, then you will need to consider the Regular Installment Agreement. There is no dollar amount limitation, but the payments cannot continue beyond the collection statute expiration. The terms of the agreement will be based upon your ability to pay and your owned assets.

The full financial disclosure documents and supporting statements are required to be submitted with the application. It is imperative here to include absolutely everything about your financial affairs. If anything is omitted and the IRS finds out, it will automatically assume you attempted concealment. The case becomes exponentially more complicated in this instance, so don't leave anything out.

It is imperative to work with an experienced and knowledgeable resolution specialist. Their job becomes positioning the client through legal strategic pre-submission planning to reduce the monthly payment amount.

The IRS has developed tables of National Standards specific to the amount of dependents you have and where you live to determine what your "allowable expenses" are. Your monthly payment is determined by the after-tax income you generate minus the allowable expenses. The trick here is to minimize your income and maximize your "allowable expenses." Taxpayers with erratic income should get professional help with the calculation to determine their monthly income.

In addition to allowable expenses, you are entitled to expenses required to maintain the health and welfare of your family. You are also allowed expenses required to generate income. I can give you a real life example of this.

CASE STUDY EXAMPLE #6 - ALLOWABLE EXPENSES

Most IRS revenue officers would not consider a live-in nanny as an allowable expense. In this case, one was allowed. This married couple had two young children and both work in the medical profession. One was an ER doctor who was required to be on call in the event additional staff was required urgently, and the other spouse was an OB-GYN who was regularly called into delivery when patients went into labor. It was a regular occurrence that they both got called into work simultaneously.

So in this case, the salary they paid to the live-in nanny was allowed as an expense because it was required both for the welfare of the family and for the production of income.

Exceptions such as this are often won by elevating the case to the Revenue Officer's Group Manager.

CLOSING THOUGHTS ABOUT INSTALLMENT AGREEMENTS

When an Offer in Compromise is not an option, the Installment Agreement is the answer for most taxpayers who want to avoid forced collections while repaying their debt on their terms. Whenever possible, the best solution is to try to qualify for the Guaranteed or Streamlined Installment Agreements. Otherwise, your best interest will be served by your tax resolution specialist minimizing your assets and income while maximizing your expenses to obtain the lowest possible payment. This keeps you in control of your monthly cash flow instead of allowing the IRS to dictate how you live and spend money.

Also keep in mind that if you are unable to pay the tax debt in full before the collection statute expiration, seriously consider the Partial Payment Installment Agreement. Sometimes this is a more favorable option than the Offer in Compromise because of the longer payment term.

12

WHAT YOU NEED TO KNOW ABOUT AUDITS

Everyone dreads the thought of getting chosen for an audit by the IRS, even if the return in question is completely accurate and legitimate.

An audit—or as the IRS calls it, *an examination*—is merely a second look at some item on the return to determine its accuracy. The majority of audits done each year are resolved by sending additional documentation or a more detailed explanation of a figure reported on the return. In more extreme cases, the entire return is called into question, but this type of audit is much less common.

In the latter case, where the entire return is examined, the IRS has far-reaching authority to delve into your entire financial life and impose additional tax, penalties, and interest if it is determined that your income or expenses were improperly reported. If you have the misfortune of being selected for this kind of exam, you need the help of a professional. By hiring a professional representative, you will never need to appear personally during the audit, and you will probably save more money on the outcome than you will pay in service fees.

How Long Does The IRS Have to Audit a Return?

The IRS has a time limit of three years from the date you filed the return to examine it. If you file before the official due date of April 15, then the three year clock starts to run on April 15.

Of course, there are exceptions to the three year rule. If a return understates income by 25% or more, then there is an additional three years added to the time limit, giving the IRS a total of six years to examine.

If you don't file a return at all or file a fraudulent return, then there is NO time limit. ALWAYS file your returns on time and NEVER file a fraudulent return.

AVOIDING AN AUDIT

A lot of taxpayers ask, **"How much can I deduct and not get audited?"** I'm sorry to say that there is no such equation. The best way I know to avoid an audit is to use a disclosure statement.

If there are any unusual items on the return, you can give a detailed explanation to the IRS by including a disclosure statement with the filing. On the disclosure statement, provide enough detail so that if the IRS has a question, the answer will be provided by reading the disclosure. If the examiner's curiosity is sufficiently satisfied, the case will be closed without additional contact with you.

One additional benefit of using a disclosure statement is to protect your return from the 3 year extension of the audit time limit in the case of a 25% or more understatement of income. Even if the income understatement on the return exceeds this threshold, the IRS only has 3 years to examine it.

WHAT ARE THE CHANCES OF BEING AUDITED?

From a statistical standpoint, the chance of your return being selected for an audit is miniscule. Less than 1% of all tax returns filed are subject to an actual audit. The chances increase based on your income level, whether you are self-employed, or if you get flagged by IRS computer programs.

Income

As your income rises, so does your incidence of audit, with the following exception: if you report no income, you are more likely to be checked than if your income exceeds six figures. Taxpayers who are hiding income typically want to hide all of it.

Self-Employed

There is a dramatic increase of audits for self-employed taxpayers. The largest division of the IRS is the Small Business/Self-Employed Division (SBSE), and they handle the highest number of audits. The IRS targets self-employed business owners who are most likely to underreport income and run personal expenses through the business.

Discriminant Inventory Function System

Computers are playing a bigger role at the IRS when targeting returns for examination. The objective is to make the most efficient use of limited human resources, so they use computer programs to help select returns with the highest potential for underpaid tax. They have a super-secret computer program called the Discriminant Inventory Function System (DIF) that assigns a "DIF number" to each return. A higher DIF number indicates a greater likelihood that the return has an underreported tax liability. Although the profession has no idea what the specific formula is, we have determined through observation that higher expense deductions relative to income gets flagged more often by the computers.

Information Returns Processing System

In addition to the DIF program, they also use the Information Returns Processing System (IRP) to double check returns for underreported income. The system compares information reported on your W-2s and 1099s to what is reported on your tax return. If they find something is missing, you will likely be getting an audit notice.

TYPES OF AUDITS

Local field offices of the IRS handle audits in one of three different ways:

- **Correspondence Audit**: They can ask for additional information through the mail.
- **Office Audit**: You may be asked to come in to the local IRS office with your documentation to discuss the return items in person.
- **Field Audit**: The worst and most intrusive audit, when the IRS comes to your place of business to conduct the audit.

CORRESPONDENCE AUDIT

The Correspondence Audit is the most common and makes up 75% of all examinations. Here, the IRS is typically questioning one of the items on your return and just needs some additional documentation to prove a deduction. The notice is sent to you through the mail and your response is returned back through the mail. Typically, no one needs to speak to you for a correspondence audit. Your best bet is to act quickly to provide clear and convincing proof of the questioned item, and be glad you didn't get selected for one of the other audits.

OFFICE AUDIT

If IRS has more questions about your return, you will be asked to attend an Office Audit. This audit is more serious and extensive. To arrange your Office Audit, the IRS will send a notice asking you to set up an appointment with the revenue officer at the local field office. As soon as you get this notice, you should contact the professional who prepared your return to represent you. Many tax preparers offer you the chance to prepay for audit representation as part of the tax preparation engagement. The fee is typically a minimal ($75 - $125) amount compared to paying for full representation after the fact. If you paid for the representation with the return, this is when it pays you back many times over. Your representative will arrange to attend the appointment *without* you. You may be asked to provide some documents, but you should not attend the audit. If there are some controversial positions on the return, you may be better off hiring someone else than the return preparer. This is to avoid having someone with a conflict of interest represent you. The preparer may "roll you under the bus" to avoid preparer penalties.

FIELD AUDIT

The Field Audit is conducted by the most experienced IRS Revenue Agents and Officers. This type of audit usually involves a business taxpayer. The agents approach the job like detectives who are trying to uncover what you may be hiding. If you give them their way, they will run roughshod through your place of business with an attitude that you are guilty until proven innocent.

Never let an IRS agent into your home unless they have a subpoena. You should do your best to keep them away from your home or business even if you have nothing to hide. They will observe the physical surroundings and can easily jump to the conclusion that you are living a lifestyle beyond the income reported on your tax return. Then it becomes your job to dispel this. It is easier to just avoid the dilemma.

In "Chapter 3: The Taxpayer Bill of Rights," you learned that you can refuse an audit at your place of business if the audit would make it impossible for you to continue your affairs. A better option would be to hire a resolution professional to represent you. Then your representative can insist that the audit should be conducted at the tax professional's office instead of your place of business.

No matter which type of audit you receive, if the controversy has the potential to be considered fraudulent, you will need an attorney to be involved to avoid your representative becoming the IRS's star witness. Only attorneys have client privilege. Your attorney may suggest working with your EA or CPA representative under a special type of agreement, called a Kovel Letter, which will extend the attorney-client privilege to the representative as well.

FINAL THOUGHTS

This chapter has offered an awareness level of information to show you how carefully to tread when dealing with an audit. The topic can easily be expanded upon to produce an entire book series. If nothing else, you should have learned to always hire a professional to represent your interest for an IRS audit.

Also consider that your tax preparer may not be specifically trained in IRS representation procedure, and is therefore less than qualified for the job. This is the time to find a tax problem resolution specialist or IRS representation specialist. In addition to the savings on the final outcome, an IRS representation specialist will never allow you to attend an audit or speak to an agent. This is to keep you from saying something that would increase your tax liability—or worse, make you subject to a criminal investigation.

AFTERWORD

The sensation you get when contacted by the IRS about a unpaid balance, whether in person or via mail, feels like a kick in the gut. When the notices keep on coming and the threats escalate, it feels even worse. Take a deep breath and remember there *is* a solution for you. If you're feeling anxious and losing sleep, relieve the stress by finding a local tax resolution specialist to fight the IRS for you. The law provides rights to taxpayers, but you typically have to stand up for them.

Most professionals will offer a no-cost initial consultation where you will discover that there is a strategy to resolve your non-compliance issues. Afterward, you will likely know how you're going to be protected from bank account seizures, wage and income garnishments, and the notice of federal tax lien. You will no longer be required to speak to the IRS, since your representative will be doing that for you. YOU will remain in control of your monthly cash flow—NOT THE IRS. You will see that you can feel good again, sleep well at night, and be more present for your family and loved ones.

You will have confidence knowing that everything is being handled properly and your family is being taken care of.

Facing the IRS head on is the best bet, but don't do it on your own. This work is meaningful and gratifying to me. I get to offer real relief to people who are suffering simply because they're unaware of their rights; I always uphold and protect my clients' rights. I get to play a key role in making their lives better and offer a fresh start towards success and prosperity. They once again are able to enjoy activities with the family and friends they love.

I take a limited number of new tax resolution cases each month. If you would like help, I encourage you to set up an appointment by contacting my office at 1-800-433-0986. You can also get started by giving us some contact information on my website (www.irscrisishelp.com), and within a day or two someone from my office will be in touch with you. If you owe less than $10,000 and need guidance on how to set up your own Guaranteed Installment Agreement, we can provide instructions.

If you have a client, friend, or family member who is struggling with a tax issue, I encourage you to share this book with them. You can play a part in helping someone get their life back.

Be Well and Prosperous,

Dirk

1-800-433-0986 (24 Hours)

www.irscrisishelp.com

ACKNOWLEDGMENTS

I must express my gratitude to Charlie Price of the Price Law Firm PLC for providing me the inspiration necessary to rise to the challenge of authoring my first book.

Larry Lawler, L.G. Brooks and Steven Klitzner of the American Society of Tax Problem Solvers (ASTPS) have been instrumental in providing me with the specialized knowledge and high standards required for taxpayer representation through their advanced educational programs and seminars. Thank you for your continuous work in elevating the standards of our profession.

Michael Rozbruch's Tax and Business Solutions Academy has helped me and numerous other professionals connect with the troubled taxpayers in need of our help. Michael, I am grateful to you for improving my life and the lives of the taxpayers whom I protect.

And a very special thank you to my high school accounting

teacher, Mrs. Sharon Dugas, who inspired me to embark upon a lifelong journey of learning.